Married Mothers in Ministry Prayer Guide

Dr. Latina C. Campbell

Copyright © 2021 Latina C. Campbell

All rights reserved. No part of this book may be reproduced in any form or by any electronic or mechanical means, including information storage and retrieval systems, without permission in writing from the publisher, except by reviewers, who may quote brief passages in a review.

ISBN: 978-1-955312-34-9

Printed in the United States of America
Story Corner Publishing & Consulting, Inc.
1510 Atlanta Ave.
Portsmouth, VA 23704

Storycornerpublishing@yahoo.com
www.StoryCornerPublishing.com

Dedication

This book is dedicated to all the women out there that feel like they cannot tell their testimony as it relates to marriage, family, and ministry. Do not hold it in any longer! Give it to God so He can heal you and make you whole.

Revelation 12:11 KJV

And they overcame him by the blood of the Lamb, and by the word of their testimony; and they loved not their lives unto the death.

Table Of Content

Introduction vi

Communication 1

Understanding 2

Self-Time 3

Keeping Martial Time Sacred 4

Feeling Overwhelmed 5

Children Are Blessings 6

In-Laws 7

Balancing Time 8

God Dwell in The Center of It All 9

Lord, Help Me to Love My Husband Your Way 10

Father, Show Us How to Parent Our Children 11

God, Please Protect My Husband 12

God, Please Protect My Children 13

Lord, Show Me Your Vision of The Ministry 14

Where Do I fit In Ministry? 15

Setting Boundaries in Our Marriage 16

Elevate Our Trust In Each Other 17

Teach Us How to Be Intimate Towards One Another 18

Lord, Show Us How to Satisfy Each Other's Sexual Needs . . 19

I Pray Against Adultery in My Marriage 20

Walking In My Calling 21

I Pray Against Competition in Ministry 22

Table Of Content

Role Models for Our Children. 23

How To Keep Our Children on Track. 24

Help Us Not to Lose Sight of Family 25

Marriage Is Our First Ministry 26

Feeling Lonely in My Marriage. 27

Misunderstood And Overlooked in Ministry 28

Sharing The Workload of Parenthood 29

Help Us to Agree as Parents. 30

Displaying You Lord 31

Patience 32

Father, I Give You All My Broken Pieces. 33

Keep The Fire Burning in My Marriage, Lord. 34

Lord, Cover and Lead the Ministry 35

Introduction

Have you ever been so stressed that you wanted to flip over a table as Yeshua did? I know I have! I have wanted to flip over several tables. Life throws things our way, and sometimes we are caught off guard. Sometimes we don't always react with a sound mind. Therefore, we always need God to help us with self-control.

This prayer guide is for all married women, with child(ren), and a part of ministry, or who plans to be in these positions. These three hats of a woman's life are tough and could be detrimental if done without God's leading. Women carry and do so much! When adding on marriage, children, and ministry, things can become overwhelming and frustrating. This prayer guide is to help reposition you at the feet of Yeshua. Only you know your life in detail and what prayers need to be answered. Allow these prayers to help you open up to God on a deeper level. God knows what you need before you ask, so don't be afraid to lay it all out to Him. He is just waiting to hear you acknowledge that you need Him, and He will come to your rescue.

Communication

James 1:19 ESV

"Know this, my beloved brothers: let every person be quick to hear, slow to speak, slow to anger;"

God,

I welcome you in to have your way in my marriage. I pray you help my husband and me to understand each other better. I know communication is essential; therefore, please improve ours. Sometimes it seems as if we are on different planets when we converse, and it can be very frustrating. Show us how to communicate and understand each other on all levels. Lord, help us to listen to one another and take into consideration the other's feelings, in Yeshua's name, Amen.

Request For God:

_____
_____
_____
_____

Understanding

Job 28:28 NIV

"And he said to the human race, "The fear of the Lord—that is wisdom, and to shun evil is understanding."

Dear God,

I want to thank you for all you are, even when you don't have to be for us. Thank you for your love, mercy, and grace. I pray you cleanse me of everything that displeases you. Help me, Holy Spirit, to be perfect and holy. Sanctify me, Holy Spirit, so that I can bring God glory in my marriage. I lift up my marriage to you, Lord, so you can have your way. God, I pray you step in when my husband and I are not seeing eye to eye. I pray you counsel each of us in our alone time to see each other through your eyes. Help us to grasp a better understanding of the areas we may disagree. Cover our marriage and continue to help us to walk together, in Yeshua's name, Amen.

Request For God:

_____
_____
_____
_____

Self-Care

1 Corinthians 6:19-20 ESV

"Or do you not know that your body is a temple of the Holy Spirit within you, whom you have from God? You are not your own, for you were bought with a price. So glorify God in your body."

Father God,

Thank you for life. It is your air that I breathe that keeps me living. I pray you add wisdom and strength to me when it comes to taking care of myself. Show me how to take time out for myself even when it doesn't seem there is time. Help me to know when I should say "no" to others and work out a schedule that includes my time. I wear so many titles and give myself to so many people in ministry and family. When I do desire to do something for myself, I'm exhausted! Reposition my perspective to put me first, in Yeshua's name, Amen.

Request For God:

_____
_____
_____
_____

Keeping Martial Time Sacred

Hebrews 13:4 ESV

"Let marriage be held in honor among all, and let the marriage bed be undefiled, for God will judge the sexually immoral and adulterous."

Lord,

Thank you for life, my husband, our children, and the opportunity to do ministry. Each day there is so much to do, but I pray that you would help me and my husband to take the time out for each other. Father, I pray that we will value our marriage above all things. I pray that we will not allow our marital time to get lost in all that we do. Show us how to keep the excitement going. Lord, please give us ideas beyond what we usually do. Shut out everything that would hinder us from spending time with one another. Hold back anyone who would attempt to stand in our way. Lord, I pray that you are pleased with our marriage, but if you are not, show us how to do better, in Yeshua's name, Amen.

Request For God:

_____

_____

_____

_____

Feeling Overwhelmed

Psalms 23:3-4 NIV

"He restores my soul. He leads me in paths of righteousness for his name's sake. Even though I walk through the valley of the shadow of death, I will fear no evil, for you are with me; your rod and your staff, they comfort me."

God,

I worship you for who you are. You are my strength, comfort, and stability. Of course, you are so much more than that to me, but today I need another dose of your strength, comfort, and peace like never before. As storms occur in my life, I know I can make it through with you by my side, adding these things unto me. Being a wife is hard, but help me to be the wife you called me. Above all, I'm honored that you called me to be a wife. Thank you for being the husband you are to me, and thank you for the husband you sent to me. When my husband and I go through things, help me keep my eyes on you, Lord, in Yeshua's name, Amen.

Request For God:

_____
_____
_____
_____

Children Are Blessings

Psalms 127:3-5 ESV

*"Behold, children are a heritage from the L*ORD*, the fruit of the womb a reward. Like arrows in the hand of a warrior are the children of one's youth. Blessed is the man who fills his quiver with them! He shall not be put to shame when he speaks with his enemies in the gate.*

God,

Please continue to cover our children. Thank you for all the children you have allowed me to birth. I am honored, although it is a lot of work. Sometimes I get overwhelmed and frustrated with the tasks of motherhood. Lord, I ask that you step in each of those moments and strengthen me. Please remind me how much of a blessing our children are when I can not think straight. Help me to appreciate being a mother, in Yeshua's name, Amen.

Request For God:

_____
_____
_____
_____

In-Laws

Mark 12:28-31 NIV

"One of the teachers of the law came and heard them debating. Noticing that Jesus had given them a good answer, he asked him, "Of all the commandments, which is the most important?" "The most important one," answered Jesus, "is this: 'Hear, O Israel: The Lord our God, the Lord is one. Love the Lord your God with all your heart and with all your soul and with all your mind and with all your strength.' The second is this: 'Love your neighbor as yourself.' There is no commandment greater than these."

Dear Heavenly Father,

You are the Most High God, and there is none other higher. There is truly none like you! No one loves me like you, Lord. No one is there for me like you, and I thank you for it. Please help me to be more like you each day. Lord, I also thank you for my husband's relatives. I thank you for adding our families together, and I give you all the glory for it. Only you could have brought us all together, and I pray the blending isn't difficult. I pray everyone respects each other and shows your love to one another. If there is difficulty blending in love and respect, I pray you break and destroy the blockage. Please soften all stony hearts and remind everyone that we are family for your purpose, in Yeshua's name, Amen.

Request For God:

_____
_____
_____
_____

Balancing Time

Ecclesiastes 3:1-8 NIV

"There is a time for everything, and a season for every activity under the heavens: a time to be born and a time to die, a time to plant and a time to uproot, a time to kill and a time to heal, a time to tear down and a time to build, a time to weep and a time to laugh, a time to mourn and a time to dance, a time to scatter stones and a time to gather them, a time to embrace and a time to refrain from embracing, a time to search and a time to give up, a time to keep and a time to throw away, a time to tear and a time to mend, a time to be silent and a time to speak, a time to love and a time to hate, a time for war and a time for peace."

Dear God,

Help me to make an effective "To-do list." I am pulled in so many different directions that I forget to do essential things. Show me what you want me to do day to day. Lord, I know you know best. Therefore, reorganize everything I have to do. Father, help me balance marriage, family, ministry, and time to myself effectively, in Yeshua's name, Amen.

Request For God:

_____

_____

_____

_____

God, Dwell in The Center of It All

Exodus 15:13 NIV

"In Your lovingkindness You have led the people whom You have redeemed; In Your strength You have guided them to Your holy habitation."

Dear Lord,

Thank you for showing us true unconditional love and sacrifice. Help us to be more like you every day. We pray our marriage will grow as we choose to love unconditionally. We also pray we will get better at surrendering everything to you. We lay our worries at your feet. Lord, we offer our thoughts, plans and submit our decisions to you. Please help us to walk in your Spirit and not in selfish ways. We pray you are glorified as we choose to draw closer to you, in Yeshua's name, Amen.

Request For God:

_____
_____
_____
_____

Lord, Help Me to Love My Husband Your Way

1 Corinthians 13:4-8 NIV

"Love is patient, love is kind. It does not envy, it does not boast, it is not proud. It does not dishonor others, it is not self-seeking, it is not easily angered, it keeps no record of wrongs. Love does not delight in evil but rejoices with the truth. It always protects, always trusts, always hopes, always perseveres. Love never fails. But where there are prophecies, they will cease; where there are tongues, they will be stilled; where there is knowledge, it will pass away."

Father God,

Thank you for your gift of love. I thank you for the sacrifice that you have made to love all your people. No one can love the way you do. Father, I pray that my husband and I will try every single day to love each other how you love us. Help us to feel loved by one another. Please remind us of what your love is every moment we stop loving each other your way. Thank you for your love that never fails us, in Yeshua's name, Amen.

Request For God:

_____

_____

_____

_____

Father, Show Us How to Parent Our Children

Deuteronomy 6:6-9 NIV

These commandments that I give you today are to be on your hearts. Impress them on your children. Talk about them when you sit at home and when you walk along the road, when you lie down and when you get up. Tie them as symbols on your hands and bind them on your foreheads. Write them on the doorframes of your houses and on your gates.

Lord,

I owe everything to you. I thank you for our children. They are indeed a gift. Please, Lord, help my husband and me raise our children the way you desire it to be done. I pray that my husband and I will only plant good seeds and impart good imprints in our children so their future can grow positive. God, I pray that you forgive us for every negative seed we have planted in our children. Please uproot and destroy every seed of darkness that has started to grow in our children so that we shall have a clean slate to plant more good seeds. God, I pray that as we teach our children all about you and your commands that you would take over and guide them all the days of their lives, in Yeshua's name, Amen.

Request For God:

_____
_____
_____
_____

God, Please Protect My Husband

Isaiah 54:17 ESV

"No weapon that is fashioned against you shall succeed, and you shall confute every tongue that rises against you in judgment. This is the heritage of the servants of the Lord and their vindication from me, declares the Lord."

Dear Father,

I pray that you hear my heart today. I thank you for being so faithful, loving, and kind. Holy Spirit, I welcome you in to have your way with my marriage. I lift up my husband to you, Lord. I pray that you bless him, strengthen him, and encourage him every day of his life. God, you know what he needs, so I pray you hear him and fulfill his needs according to your will. I pray that you cover and protect him as the head of our household and, most importantly, my head. Help me to love him with your love every moment, in Yeshua's name, Amen.

Request For God:

_____
_____
_____
_____

God, Please Protect My Children

Isaiah 41:10 ESV

"Fear not, for I am with you; be not dismayed, for I am your God; I will strengthen you, I will help you, I will uphold you with my righteous right hand."

Father God,

Thank you for the lives of our children. I pray that your Holy Spirit guild them in all their ways. Please cover and protect them from hurt, harm, and danger seen and unseen. Send your warring angels to go before them and to take charge over them. God, I pray you keep our children in your hands and don't let them go, in Yeshua's name, Amen.

Request For God:

_____

_____

_____

_____

Lord, Show Me Your Vision of The Ministry

Acts 20:24 NIV

"However, I consider my life worth nothing to me; my only aim is to finish the race and complete the task the Lord Jesus has given me—the task of testifying to the good news of God's grace."

Lord,

Only you know the plans for the ministry. Please reveal the vision so I can follow. Lord, show my husband the vision of the ministry as well. I desire to show your people your son Jesus Christ through everything I do. I pray the ministry is being carried out the way you desire it to be. If not, please send correction, in Yeshua's name, Amen.

Request For God:

_____

_____

_____

_____

Where Do I fit In Ministry?

John 15:18-20 NIV

"If the world hates you, keep in mind that it hated me first. If you belonged to the world, it would love you as its own. As it is, you do not belong to the world, but I have chosen you out of the world. That is why the world hates you. Remember what I told you: 'A servant is not greater than his master. If they persecuted me, they will persecute you also. If they obeyed my teaching, they will obey yours also."

God,

I find myself as the outcast in ministry. I am overlooked, disrespected, and not honored at all. Many attending the ministry only see my husband and maybe our children. For the most part, no one sees me. Not that I care about being in the forefront, I just want to be respected. Please show me my place in all this outside of being a wife and mother. Do I just sit and smile? Do I try to speak to your people? Or do I just pray for them all? Please give me peace and push my husband to reenforce respect boundaries when he sees the people stepping out of line, in Yeshua's name, Amen.

Request For God:

_____
_____
_____
_____

Setting Boundaries in Our Marriage

1 Thessalonians 3:12 NIV

"May the Lord make your love increase and overflow for each other and for everyone else, just as ours does for you."

Dear God,

I know you are a healer and a deliverer because I have seen it before. Thank you so much for working in my life the way you do. I lift up my in-laws and the ministry members to you. I ask that you bless, heal, and deliver each of them according to your will. Sometimes we do not get along because they overstep boundaries in my marriage. It drives to me contemplate disconnecting from them, but I know I cannot fully shut them out. Lord you know all, and you see all. Please help me to keep calm in those situations and allow you to take control. I pray you push my husband to cover me and to reenforce our marriage boundaries in those moments. Holy Spirit I pray in those times you bring reconciliation for everyone without delay. I pray you help us all to respect and love each other on one accord with your will, in Yeshua's name, Amen.

Request For God:

_____

_____

_____

_____

Elevate Our Trust In Each Other

2 Samuel 22:31 KJV

"As for God, his way is perfect; the word of the Lord is tried: he is a buckler to all them that trust in him."

Lord,

Thank you for connecting my husband and I together. Please continue to take our love deep in you. I pray we trust each other at another level each day. Help us to trust each other to the point that no one else could come between us. Show us how to walk in unison without fear and doubt in each other, in Yeshua's name, Amen.

Request For God:

_____
_____
_____
_____

Teach Us How to Be Intimate Towards One Another

Genesis 2:24-25 AMPC

"Therefore, a man shall leave his father and his mother and shall become united and cleave to his wife, and they shall become one flesh. And the man and his wife were both naked and were not embarrassed or ashamed in each other's presence."

Dear Lord,

I thank you for my marriage. Holy Spirit I welcome you in to teach us how to connect on a deeper level every day. I pray that the fire never burns out concerning our intimacy. If it has, Lord you be the fire and light it again. I pray that every time we lay eyes upon each other we would remember how you connected us together. Our love would also grow and cause our hearts to skip a beat. I pray that my husband and I remain faithful to growing with each other that we become completely in sync with each other. I want to read him even when I am not trying. Most importantly, I pray you are pleased with our marriage. If you are not pleased, show us how to make it right in your sight, in Yeshua's name, Amen.

Request For God:

_____
_____
_____
_____

Lord, Show Us How to Satisfy Each Other's Sexual Needs

1 Corinthians 7:3-5 ESV

"The husband should give to his wife her conjugal rights, and likewise the wife to her husband. For the wife does not have authority over her own body, but the husband does. Likewise the husband does not have authority over his own body, but the wife does. Do not deprive one another, except perhaps by agreement for a limited time, that you may devote yourselves to prayer; but then come together again, so that Satan may not tempt you because of your lack of self-control."

Father God,

You know all that goes on intimately in our marriage. Some days is good, and others are not so good. Sometimes there is enough time and other times there is not. Sex is an important part of our marriage, but sometimes there is lack. Lord, I pray you not only show my husband and I how to satisfy each other but help us to prioritize sex. Remind us that sex is an act that spiritually makes us one. Thank you for the oneness that transpires through sex with my husband. Every time we have sex, please manifest closeness, agreement, and unity I our marriage, in Yeshua's name, Amen.

Request For God:

_____

_____

_____

_____

I Pray Against Adultery in My Marriage

Deuteronomy 22:22

"If a man is found lying with a married woman, then both of them shall die, the man who lay with the woman, and the woman; thus you shall purge the evil from Israel."

Heavenly Father,

Please cover my marriage. I pray you continue to keep my husband and I. Help us to stay committed to you and each other. Father, I pray you reveal every secret, lie, and any intruders in my marriage. Lord, please vindicate on my behalf. If my husband or I is out of alinement, get us back in order, in Yeshua's name, Amen.

Request For God:

_____
_____
_____
_____

Walking In My Calling

Ephesians 4:1-6

"As a prisoner for the Lord, then, I urge you to live a life worthy of the calling you have received. Be completely humble and gentle; be patient, bearing with one another in love. Make every effort to keep the unity of the Spirit through the bond of peace. There is one body and one Spirit, just as you were called to one hope when you were called; one Lord, one faith, one baptism; one God and Father of all, who is over all and through all and in all."

God,

I thank you for choosing me to do the work of your Kingdom. I am honored but nervous at the same time. I do not want to disappoint you so please show me all the details of how to complete my assignment. I know you did not give me the spirit of fear, therefore, help me to walk boldly in the calling you chose for me, in Yeshua's name, Amen.

Request For God:

_____
_____
_____
_____

I Pray Against Competition in Ministry

2 Corinthians 10:12 NIV

"Not that we dare to classify or compare ourselves with some of those who are commending themselves. But when they measure themselves by one another and compare themselves with one another, they are without understanding."

Heavenly Father,

Thank you for the ministry you have entrusted to my husband and I. Show us how to walk in agreement side by side and not in competition. Help us to see that we need each other because there are certain things, he cannot do that I can and vice versa. Remind us that we are not a threat to each other, but should be helping each other, in Yeshua's name, Amen.

Request For God:

_____
_____
_____
_____

Role Models for Our Children

Proverbs 22:6 NIV

"Start children off on the way they should go, and even when they are old they will not turn from it."

Father God,

Thank you for the gift of marriage and family. I know that my husband and I influence each other and our children. Sometimes in good ways and sometimes in bad. I pray we would be intentional to walk in the Spirit and not in our flesh, so that we could influence each other and our children how you desire us. Help us to encourage each other and help build one another up as we set examples for each other and our children every day by the way we choose to live. Holy Spirit please take control, in Yeshua's name, Amen.

Request For God:

_____
_____
_____
_____

How To Keep Our Children on Track

Proverbs 29:17 NIV

"Discipline your children, and they will give you peace; they will bring you the delights you desire."

Lord,

The world has so much corruption going on that it gets overwhelming at times. Sometimes I wonder if I'm doing a good enough job as a mother. It is so easy for our children to get sucked into the traps of the enemy that I worry. Lord, please show us how to keep our children focused on you. Holy Spirit, help our children to live a holy and righteous life, in Yeshua's name, Amen.

Request For God:

_____
_____
_____
_____

Help Us Not to Lose Sight of Family

Proverbs 17:6 NIV

"Children's children are a crown to the aged, and parents are the pride of their children."

Dear God,

I pray that you help my husband and I to prioritize better. Help us to never lose sight of family being first before anything. I pray that ministry never overshadows family time. I pray our businesses, career, or jobs do not take away from investing in our family. As we supply the needs for people, places, and things, I pray we never forget the needs of our children and each other. I pray our family is the way you want us to be and if we are not, please shift us into alinement. Push our family bond deeper, help us to pray more together, stay on one accord, and to love each other how you love us. Help my husband and I to be available when our children need us. Show us how to enjoy being a family that you called us to be, in Yeshua's name, Amen.

Request For God:

_____
_____
_____
_____

Marriage Is Our First Ministry

Ephesians 5:33 NIV

"However, let each one of you love his wife as himself, and let the wife see that she respects her husband."

Lord,

Thank you for my husband. Sometimes life gets so routine, and we go about our days and forget to pray for one another. I forget to pray for his needs, heart, and mind. I pray for him right now and ask that you protect him from the attacks of the enemy. Please fill him with joy and peace. Cover our marriage and soak us in your precious blood. Help me not to forget prayer for my husband and marriage which is so essential and necessary. Show me how to be my husband's helper and what to pray for him daily. Please bless my husband and our marriage beyond our dreams. Mature us in every area of our marriage, in Yeshua's name, Amen.

Request For God:

_____
_____
_____
_____

Feeling Lonely in My Marriage

Psalms 32:7 NIV

"You are a hiding place for me; you preserve me from trouble; you surround me with shouts of deliverance. Selah"

God,

I thank you for always hearing my cry. You are worthy to be praised. You always know what I need when I am in need. Father, I pray you would invade my marriage and set everything in order, including my husband and me. I have been feeling disconnected and lonely in my marriage. God, I know marriage is supposed to be the two become one; therefore, push us together to create one. I am tired of the way things have been and it gets me discouraged at times. Please show us on behalf of my marriage and do what needs to be done, in Yeshua's name, Amen.

Request For God:

_____
_____
_____
_____

Misunderstood And Overlooked in Ministry

Psalms 34:17-18 NIV

"The righteous cry out, and the LORD hears them; he delivers them from all their troubles. The LORD is close to the brokenhearted and saves those who are crushed in spirit."

Lord,

As the wife of my husband, many in ministry overlook me. They pretend as if I am invisible and do not respect me. God, please help me to continue in love when I have thoughts of walking away from the church. Help me to be humble and remember everything should be about pleasing you. Please cover and protect my husband from everyone who preys on him. Also, raise my discernment to see people and things for what they really are, in Yeshua's name, Amen.

Request For God:

_____
_____
_____
_____

Sharing The Workload of Parenthood

Proverbs 1:8-9 NIV

"Listen, my son, to your father's instruction and do not forsake your mother's teaching. They are a garland to grace your head and a chain to adorn your neck."

Lord,

I praise you for who you are. You are a way-maker and so much more to me and my family. Thank you for my husband. Thank you for allowing us to parent your children. At times they can be a lot of work. Please help my husband and I to always work together. Show us how to help each other when in need. Step in when we become overwhelmed and comfort us, in Yeshua's name, Amen.

Request For God:

_____
_____
_____
_____

Help Us to Agree as Parents

1 Corinthians 1:10 NIV

"*I appeal to you, brothers and sisters, in the name of our Lord Jesus Christ, that all of you agree with one another in what you say and that there be no divisions among you, but that you be perfectly united in mind and thought.*"

God,

Thank you for giving my husband and I wonderful children. I pray you continue to cover and guild them. Father sometimes it is hard for my husband and I to raise them because of our different styles of parenting. We were both raised differently, therefore we tend to disagree a lot when it comes to our children. Please help us to raise our children the way you purposed. Show us how to walk in agreement in all areas of our life, in Yeshua's name, Amen.

Request For God:

_____

_____

_____

_____

Displaying You Lord

Galatians 5:22-23 NIV

"But the fruit of the Spirit is love, joy, peace, forbearance, kindness, goodness, faithfulness, gentleness and self-control. Against such things there is no law."

Father God,

I pray for more understanding of who you are so that my husband and I may display you better. Please help me to understand your Word and the importance of every scripture in the Bible. I pray your truth would saturate our heart. Please fill me and my husband with your wisdom. I pray to gain knowledge and grasp a better understanding of your Will for our life and marriage, in Yeshua's name, Amen.

Request For God:

_____
_____
_____
_____

Patience

Ecclesiastes 7:8-9 NIV

"The end of a matter is better than its beginning, and patience is better than pride. Do not be quickly provoked in your spirit, for anger resides in the lap of fools."

God,

I pray you help me trust you more. I pray that I would be confident in your Will, ways, and plans for my life. Please give me more patience to follow your plans through until the end. I pray other husbands and wives would also be confident in you purpose and Will for them also. Help us to trust your leading even when it doesn't make sense. I pray we would rely on you and come to you for everything, in Yeshua's name, Amen.

Request For God:

_____
_____
_____
_____

Father, I Give You All My Broken Pieces

Psalms 91:9-16 ESV

"Because you have made the LORD *your dwelling place— the Most High, who is my refuge— no evil shall be allowed to befall you, no plague come near your tent. For he will command his angels concerning you to guard you in all your ways. On their hands they will bear you up, lest you strike your foot against a stone. You will tread on the lion and the adder; the young lion and the serpent you will trample underfoot. ..."*

Lord,

Thank you for my life, husband, children, and ministry. Thank you for love and joy. I pray you bless every area of my life today. Please guard and protect everything connected to from the enemy and his flaming arrows. I give you all my broken pieces to mend them back together like only you can. Show me how to be humbler and mature in my marriage. Show me how to go deeper in you and ministry. Please awaken my children to give you all the glory and praise. Heal me, restore me, and use me, in Yeshua's name, Amen.

Request For God:

_____
_____
_____
_____

Keep The Fire Burning in Our Marriage, Lord

Romans 12:11-12 NIRV

"Never let the fire in your heart go out. Keep it alive. Serve the Lord. When you hope, be joyful. When you suffer, be patient. When you pray, be faithful."

Lord,

I thank you for my husband. Thank you for the wonderful gift you have given to me. God, I pray that you help me to always value my husband as a gift, even when I do not want to. Forgive me Father for the times that I have mishandled the gift you have given me. Help me to fall in love with my husband more and more each day. I pray that I will be excited about my gift every moment. Lord, help me to carry the same zeal and fire in my heart that I had when I first fell in love with him. I pray that moment replays repeatedly in my mind no matter what. I pray my husband would look at me the same, in Yeshua's name, Amen.

Request For God:

_____
_____
_____
_____

Lord, Cover and Lead the Ministry

Psalms 91:4 NLT

"He will cover you with his feathers. He will shelter you with his wings. His faithful promises are your armor and protection."

Father God,

Thank you for never leaving us. Thank you for your wisdom. Lord, I pray that you would take hold of our ministry and guide us in what to do. We honor you as Lord and our keeper. Please show us the vision for the ministry and help us to carry it out without compromise. Thank you for trusting us with your people. Continue to protect them and us from the evil one, in Yeshua's name, Amen.

Request For God:

_____
_____
_____
_____

www.ingramcontent.com/pod-product-compliance
Lightning Source LLC
Chambersburg PA
CBHW071424070526
44578CB00003B/682